T.A.G.G.E.D. U.R. IT!

Become the Leader of Your Own Life

By: RiTika Rose

This book is dedicated to everyone that has been presented in my life. You have all been my teachers and I thank you!

To the City of Angels - I AM Honored.

Bay Area this story has started and ended with you.

Thank you dear family, friends, and clients who have given your support to this book.

Look forward to the rest of the journey.

With Love.

Contents

Introduction

I'm here today to tell you that you've been Tagged. And U R It! Now is your time to become consciously awakened to your true authentic self that otherwise may be holding you back. I think today of the Great Solar Eclipse that happened as I'm finishing the writing of this book, and it really reminds me of how I had lived my life for many years. I had lived my "previous" life with my light hidden behind the darkness. Although people saw me as happy, joyful, strong, independent, always dancing to my own tune, which I was, I knew inside that my light wasn't shining into the world as they saw it. I was battling the internal conversation of why my life wasn't looking like somebody else's or how society wanted it to be vs being ok to just be me. It was like I was living two lives. My inner and outer worlds were not connected, which no one could see or understand.

Do you ever feel that way? Are you detached from other people's opinions, in-

cluding your own? Or are you so connected to those opinions that you can't
come to a place of living and being your
true self? Are you angry, anxious, or depressed? Do you take accountability for
your life, its happiness and your inner
peace? Or do you allow your peace and
happiness to be dictated by the ideas
and concerns of others? When did you
become unhappy, distrusting or cynical
towards your life and your world? When
did you learn it was not ok to just be
you?

As a child, teenager, and even young
adult (sometimes now too as an adult) I
went through rejection, teasing and
judgment. I felt society and peer pres-
sures that did not feel right to me. I
know what it feels like to not be accepted. To have people say things about you
that, not just sting, but they stick. You
can take those on as your personal view
of yourself and even though you know it
is not true, they become your truth. I
lived that way for many years. And I
know as you're reading this you may be
there too.

These "unhappy" experiences left a huge residue of inner conflict to my mind body and soul. This internal conversation of not being good enough carried on into my adult years, although very successful in many areas, I still never fully loved or accepted myself until I became highly self-realized through a profound spiritual awakening that shifted my world and way of being forever.

As I write this book now, it's hard to even remember who I was or what I felt like 7 years ago. I stopped complaining and started living. I started taking responsibility for my life instead of putting it in the hands of others. It is such an uplift, it is so freeing and it helps you feel so powerful to stand and live in your own truth.

So What Happened?

One night after being absolutely done with the way my life was progressing, on my knees desperate to understand my life and its purpose and why all these experiences were happening "to me", I tell people that is when God roared in and set me on my path of personal and spiritual development that has taught me many more lessons about our purpose and conscious living. These lessons shifted my relationship with myself and others, as well as my career path. I practiced techniques and steps to keep my life consistently peaceful, happy, and balanced. I realized all was being done "for me" so I could enlighten myself and grow into my purpose that I now share with others and within my integrative healing and life coaching practice. I have been guided to write this book on these simple steps that you can incorporate into your life on a daily basis. Because life really and truly is meant to be simple. I hope these steps can help bring a level of peace and simplicity to your daily life, as it has mine. I want you to know that you have the hope of creating internal lasting happiness, love, peace and joy.

On this journey together, my intention for you is to reflect, learn, grow and find the areas to incorporate into your daily practice that will help make major shifts in your personal, professional and social life just like it did in mine. It was a whirlwind of unfolding for me, yet I found myself in my true, authentic, balanced, peaceful self not just on the outside as people "saw" me, but *most importantly* on the inside as well. This is what I want for you.

As I found a deeper connection to my God source (others may call this higher power, universal power, source or creator) I started seeing myself as the light that God sees me in, that's when everything changed. I was now becoming aware of how loved, beautiful and perfect we all are, because God has a purpose for all of us. That's when my truth about myself and others changed. That's when I found acceptance of myself, others and my circumstances.

Being thankful for all things big and small, realizing how much I was giving and not receiving back, knowing how I was communicating with people and how I was receiving communication, and where I let myself be attached to things that were hindering me from moving forward, that's where I found my light. Through that, I realized it is up to me to take responsibility for myself. It didn't matter what anybody else thought of me, what society thought of me, what the community thought, where I wasn't progressing or being a way that others thought I needed to. That didn't matter because my purpose and my mission was to be fulfilled in my time. Everything that I was moving through was a lesson for me to learn in order to take the next steps to enlightening myself, loving myself and becoming the person that I'm meant to be.

In truth, all is perfect, whole and complete right now. You can rest assured your life is on purpose for a purpose.

Let's become conscious of this and transform into the being that you were always meant to be. This is a journey that we'll take together because, now that you are tagged, you are it.

T.A.G.G.E.D. U.R. I.T. are eight life mastery skills I learned through my conscious awakening. These are the eight skills I realized I wasn't practicing on a daily basis, and it was holding me back from living my best life, my happiest and most authentic self. Let me break that down for you:

T= Truth

A= Acceptance

G= Gratitude

G= Giving and Receiving

E= Expression

D= Detachment

U= Unconditional Love

R= Responsibility

(Resulting in)

IT= Internal Transformation

When I realized I was really starting to practice these eight skills on a daily basis and really incorporating them into my life and my consciousness, the level of inner peace, happiness and joy that I felt, it wasn't just superficial. It was a deep happiness, a deep joy, a deep peace within myself, for others, and for the world that I was in.

Of course it didn't come overnight. It all came with learning, practice and growth but then it all just sort of came together as one, and as a way of being. As I mentioned there were major shifts in my personal and professional life and most importantly with relationship to myself and others. People were seeing changes in me. People were asking me "How do you stay so positive? How have you become such a peaceful being? How are you so open? We've never met anybody like you." I was impacting more and more people positively with my "new" way of being. That's what we are going to do together for you.

Because, ultimately, in the end we are responsible for becoming the leaders of our own life.

Let's begin.

T = Truth

"No one is you and that is your Power"

— Dave Grohl

When I came to the realization and understanding that everyone, including my self is created for their unique personal purpose that they are meant to serve, it shifted my mindset into power being because I knew now that our life wasn't created just to live. It was created so we can live our purpose. While remembering that you're created on purpose and for a purpose the first thing to remember then is to always be true to yourself.

Being true to yourself means following your inner truth, honoring and keeping integrity to yourself and your inner "knowing" and not being influenced by the outside world on how we are to be and do. When we're influenced from the outside world, then we're not operating from an authentic place, that's where we tend to build up the emotions that don't serve us such as anger, anxiety, fear or depression. That's how we end up with a lack of purpose and fulfillment in the world. A sense of not really being, or really knowing who you are because you are not truly being who you are and using the gifts and qualities only you can bring to the world.

What we have got to remember about our truth is that, everyone operates based on their own experiences. And those experiences are on purpose for us. So, how we're "being" is based on our experiences in life and that is absolutely okay. Our experiences are for us to have in order to help us and move us forward through the lessons that we are supposed to learn along our soul's journey. Our journey is unique in itself, just as everyone else's journey is unique for them. Everyone is sitting in their own present moment truth based on what life has presented to them thus far.

There are no accidents in our truth. How we look, how we live, who our family is, the circumstances life has led us on. This is all part of our soul's journey.

Each uniquely crafted so we may learn, grow, heal, and develop into who we are divinely created to be. How we choose to let these truths effect our thoughts or our thoughts of others is what will create how we feel, how we are being, and the experience we have in life and with one another.

What is it that you know to be true about your thoughts, feelings, and emotions? What truly makes you happy when it comes to your morals, ethics, activities, people, and things? Do you stay in touch with your truth? Or are you conforming to others to make them happy so you may fit in or not be rejected by others? Who told you it was not okay to be you and only you? Who told you that the experiences you were having or that the circumstances of your life are not the way that they should be or that they were not okay by society? Where and when did you create the thought process that who you truly are was not good enough? What life experiences did you have that lead you to believe this?

When we remember that we have been created uniquely and purposefully to fulfill our divine path, with no mistake, no accident and no judgment, just pure love form, we can then sit in a peace knowing that we are a unique beauty and expression of self, aligned with divine light and placed here to deliver our uniqueness to this earth.

In pureness, all is truth and love because all living things were created through truth, love and divine purity. There is no good or bad, no right and wrong. Everything is just a purposeful experience meant to be had and learned so that you can evolve into your enlightened path. So you see, standing in your truth and being who you are is an integral part of your happiness and your life's purpose, as well as your inner peace.

It is this truth that is going to set you on your purpose. Once you are operating within your purpose, you will begin to experience the joys of fulfillment.

Take a moment right now and reflect on the times you have said or done certain things that did not feel true to yourself. How did it make you feel? Physically? Emotionally? What else manifested into your life that was not producing a happy or satisfying experience because you chose a path that was not honoring your true self.

Think about a time you stood your ground and honored yourself and your true beliefs. How did that feel? What magically appeared or was created because you sat in your truth?

Next time someone irritates you, or you judge them, take a moment prior to reacting and remind yourself that this is the experience and journey that person is currently on. This is the truth they know in this present moment. Allow them to learn, heal, and grow from it. We cannot change or force another person's process, *yet* we may be sent to each other for the process.

Also ask yourself why are you judging or criticizing someone? What area in your life does not feel powerful or secure? What are you actually judging about yourself? Where can you step into your personal, truth, purpose, and power? What can you actually learn about or from this person? Choosing how you react will ultimately be part of your experience, lesson and journey as well as your level of peace and happiness.

Think about how it feels to argue with someone who is just not seeing your side. Have you been on the opposite side of the coin and you just don't see the other person's point of view? Think about why that is? Could it be based on your knowledge, experiences, and what you have been taught up to that point is the truth you know to be?

The other person, also has their own set of experiences that have led them to their version of their truth up until that point.

It may not be something you agree with, they may not agree with you, what we can do is remember to meet everyone where they are, knowing there journey is still unfolding, as is yours.

When you start to be at peace with standing in your own truth and trusting in yourself and your inner knowing, you can then start the process of fully accepting yourself and others.

A big part of my teasing growing up was about my "big" nose. This teasing went on through all my school years. People would even come up to me and ask me why I don't get plastic surgery. Can you imagine? In my hearts of hearts I knew changing myself for the sake of others was not right. I remember the day I decided I was beautiful and didn't let the words and teasing affect me anymore. I carried myself different. I respected and loved myself differently. That was when just like that people started complementing me, my beauty, and even my nose and how beautiful my nose was to them! Who would have thunk it!? With that one mind shift, all that hatred I remember as a child diminished. That's right, I am a unique beautiful being, just like you! What are you not going to allow effect you anymore?

A = Acceptance

"Acceptance doesn't prohibit growth, rather it fosters it."

- Marianne Williamson

Once you're sitting in your truth, knowing that it's okay to be just where you are and who you are, then you can start accepting yourself. Through the process of accepting yourself you also start to accept and forgive others because you now understand that they're also living their own truth through their own story. It is essentially taking away any judgment you have of yourself and others, which is a symptom for stress, lack of peace and unhappiness.

What does it mean to accept?

Acceptance literally means "willingness to tolerate". Do you ever question how you can possibly accept something that feels so wrong? Or question if someone will accept you fully and truly for who you are? Do you have trouble accepting others for who they are or what they do?

Remembering that all is happening on purpose for a purpose could you possibly see every situation as the truth of this present moment? You can choose any situation and label it as wrong or unaccepting. Or you can choose to shift your perspective and accept the situation as it is in that moment because the present moment is really all there is, the truth of that moment.

You ask yourself then, if every moment is the truth, and the truth always has its purpose, how is this situation actually serving you? How are we learning and growing from this experience or situation? What lesson is it teaching you about yourself or others?

Whether it feels good or not, you have the power to self-reflect on why the situation or person is effecting you the way that it is. When you come to a place where you can accept everything as it is in this present moment, you can make a proactive choice to observe the situation, have less negative reaction to it and take responsibility for making shifts ensuring the best outcomes for overall peace and happiness.

When we do not accept something, we usually put up a fight against it which, sit for a moment and reflect, does not promote happiness, peace or joy. Fighting only highlights anger and fear. So let's question now, what are you not accepting? What are you fighting against? Are you not happy with your job, financial situations, friends, family, partners, yourself? What are you not accepting about yourself or others in the situation?

We cannot fully accept other people and situations, if we don't come to a place of accepting ourselves first. When you do not accept yourself for who you uniquely are, you end up fighting against your true nature and being. The soul can never feel settled in this stage. Accepting yourself will allow you to stand in your power, truth and unique self, which will then allow you to open up to accepting others for their unique gifts and qualities as well. Standing in your power and truth, in full acceptance of yourself and situations will help you to start leading decisions that are best for you overall, instead of following alongside the ride of others, or worrying about what others think.

Once we have come to a place of accepting ourselves and everyone in all situations that is the only thing that we start to see. We can start forgiving ourselves and others because we accept ourselves and others for the place we were when we were not our best selves. We understand there is still soul level learning and growth to be had. All of the other un-serving stuff that is angering us, frustrating us, turning into judgment, anxiety or gossip and not allowing us to accept what is, will eventually wash away.

It is rather simple you see, something that triggers our emotion is just highlighting an unresolved conflict within ourselves. This triggered emotion allows us to step into ourselves and evaluate, what was the unpleasant experience that

I had in the past that has not been re-solved, that is reminding me of it now in this current situation? This will answer your question as to why something is hard for you to accept.

When we allow ourselves to step out of the present moment, which is the only reality, we are then worrying about the future which is anxiety or we are worrying about something that happened in the past which is depression. Neither of these feelings are ones that ever feel good to the soul.

Can you think of a time that you were ever feeling anxious about something? How did it make you feel? How did it actually stop you from moving forward or experiencing the moment?

How about depression? Can you remember a time when you were feeling depressed? Worrying about something that happened in the past a year ago, a month ago, even a day ago. How did you feel when your thoughts were lingering about something that had already happened, already been done?

The only thing that can be done in the moment is to focus on the present moment. Be in acceptance of what has already happened. What is the now of this moment? What can you do in this present moment to help shift or resolve any un-serving thoughts or feelings? What can you focus on that is beautiful and perfect in this moment?

We have choice about our mindset and actions. The beauty is we get to choose how our thoughts unfold. When we look at all situations as ones that have come our way purposefully, that have allowed us to grow, learn, and expand ourselves, instead of not accepting things as they have come to us or as we allowed things to be, we can then start to feel thankful for the experiences that are helping us gain wisdom and insight into ourselves and the world around us. Forgive yourself and others for any areas that have felt less than. Be grateful for the growth it has provided for you in the bigger plan. In the end, acceptance and forgiveness enables your peace of mind.

One of my favorite testimonials is from a client who sent her mother to me for a session. Mom had forgotten her truth and thus was not accepting herself, others and her current circumstances. She was feeling judged by society for her personal spiritual views, which was taking away her power in being ok with herself and her beliefs. We got to the root of it, the purpose behind this lesson, and discovered the way to move forward resulting in deeper peace around accepting herself and her processes just as it is. "RiTika brought my mom out of a 5 years depression in 60 minutes! I am so grateful!"

G = Gratitude

"If the only prayer you ever say is Thank You that would be enough"

— Eckhart Tolle

Choosing gratitude in every situation can and will surely shift you into happiness and a better version of you!

What does gratitude mean? Gratitude means accepting all things, people, experiences that come your way. Because, without them, as you just read, we cannot learn, grow, expand into the people we individually are supposed to become. Life has not presented itself to be hard, torturous, sad and depressing. At our birthright, life has been given to us so we can shine, enjoy, love, be free and be joyous of all the beauty that is around us.

When I started living through gratitude and being thankful for every little thing that has come my way ("good" or "bad") and also realizing nothing has to be given to me and anything can be taken away in any moment, it shifts your mindset to truly be thankful for what you have been given and what you have learnt about yourself and others.

When you take a moment, a present moment and think about all that you are thankful for, things, people, experiences, that without them, your life wouldn't be what it is today. How happy does it make you feel? Water, flowers, cool breeze, warmth, the sun, mother, father, husband, wife, children, job, finances, we can even be thankful for toilets and toothpaste. Yes, even the not so pleasant experiences such as spite, gossip, divorce, death, surgery, etc., we can be thankful for. Why? Because, still without those experiences we would not build our strength, wisdom, integrity, endurance, or depth of understanding people, ourselves, and life without it.

So many things that we have been given that make our lives easier, happier, better, more wise, compassionate, forgiving and stronger as a human and spiritual being.

Why then do we choose to think about anything that is not making our lives happier or better? When we choose distracting, un-serving thoughts, what is that doing to us? Putting us back into depression or anxiety. That's no fun!

What do you have now that without it life could be worse? What can you be grateful for right now, that without it, you would not be comfortable? What can you appreciate now that is making your life more uplifting?

Forget about for a moment what it is you think you need and should have had, it is moot point for this present moment. Just focus on what you have that serves you, that has helped you grow, that has propelled you into who you are today.

Whether you have viewed it as good experience, bad experience, challenging experience, take time to self-reflect. Ask yourself and practice being grateful for how these situations helped you better your life, better who you are, better your relationships with the lessons you learned from them.

Take time to reflect and be grateful for how these situations helped you to understand what you want and don't want in your life, who you want and don't want in your life, what consciously sits well with you and doesn't. How have these situations shifted the person you want to be?

When we sit in thankfulness, remembering that there are no accidents, only messages and lessons ordered divinely to help us grow and be the best person we can be, we can start to embrace and view all experiences as constructive feedback and begin being grateful for them. Guess what happens? We begin to say thank you to others for all experiences "good' or "bad". We start to feel a greater gratitude for all people and things. We start to see our inner and outer world more peacefully and thankfully. Every day becomes Thanksgiving Day. Every day, every hour, every minute, becomes that one that is to be thankful for. Oh what a feeling!

Take a look around you right now, or turn within yourself and think about all things you are grateful for.

Pick up the phone, send an email, set up a time to thank someone or many others in your life that you NOW see as being a divine gift. Say thank you in person for how they helped to shift your life. If it is someone that has passed on or far away, you can energetically send a thank you by simply saying it in your mind to that person or out loud as you desire.

Up until college, I don't remember ever saying thank you to a compliment given to me. I didn't believe it. One day an ex-boyfriend said to me. "You never say thank you when I compliment you" That was an eye opener. I didn't realize it. I then became very conscious of saying thank you whenever I was acknowledged, because I realized the other party truly was wanting to appreciate me, and by ignoring it I wasn't appreciating myself. And same goes for you. Not only do I thank the personal acknowledgements, I literally say thank you to everything that has come my way or that is coming my way. Every message or conversation I have I end off with a Thank you, because everything that we receive is a blessing. Stay in gratitude and receive the gratitude.

G = Giving and Receiving

"The balance of giving and receiving is essential to keeping your energy, mood and motivation at a consistently high level"

— Doreen Virtue

Another beautiful gift we have that can be worked together with gratitude is giving. There is an energetic law confirming the exchange of giving back once receiving. Without, we as people, and internally within ourselves will create an imbalance. For everything we receive, we must give back. We cannot just take from another without an exchange of showing gratitude through giving back. Without reciprocation, an energy block is created between the sources.

The importance of giving comes from the understanding that without reciprocating for what you have been given, you will not find value or regard for what you have received. The importance of receiving comes from valuing yourself and your gifts enough to allow yourself an equal energy exchange to promote balance, peace and joy.

Being a giver by nature, I realized I was not giving back to myself or allowing myself to receive from others in a way that would keep my life balanced. I would tend to handle things on my own, go out of my way to be there for others and help others, not always receiving back as much as I was giving. Does this sound like you? Once I started to value myself and my time, I learnt to start asking for help and support. (And I was surprised as to how many people actually want to help and support!) I learnt to allow myself to receive via reiki, massages, manicures or someone making me dinner. I also learnt the value of receiving alone time for all the people time I was giving by going to sit by the water on my own, watching a movie on my own, or going for a walk by myself. I learnt to value the services I provide and ask for the monetary amount the service was worth or love donations in some aspects to honor myself for what I was giving. It shifted my energy field because I was now allowing a healthy balance to flow.

Think back for a moment now when you, at some point in your life, just gave and gave and gave to another person or through your work and felt it was totally one sided on your part. How did that make you feel? Did you feel resentment? Tired? Ready to throw in the towel? Even though I am sure you were happy to do it and worked so hard to support or get the job done, some gesture or acknowledgment from the other party would have balanced out the giving that was done.

Keeping this in mind, were you ever that receiver in a situation? What was holding you back from giving back to the source you were receiving from? Generally when we do not or cannot value another, somewhere internally we are not valuing ourselves. Where do you still need to feel validated by others that you can only seem to take and not give back? Are there areas of truth and acceptance about yourself that you are not embracing and still struggling with?

Giving does not have to always go directly back to the person. Not all people desire receiving directly. Sometimes it can be giving back to their cause or someone that is important to them. With an understanding, this can be an exchange of energy.

For example, Mother Teresa and her honorable works for the poverty stricken. Here is a woman that gave her life for her work and to ensure a better life for others. She did not ask for anything in return except for those to give to the people she was helping and serving. That was giving back enough for her.

Others bring a bottle of wine to someone's home to thank them for having them over. It may not be an equal exchange but it is an exchange of gratitude and acknowledgement nonetheless.

There are now employee appreciation days, boss days, secretary days etc. that will allow giving back to someone who is giving so much to others.

The most common is pay for services or pay for an item. That is an energy exchange. Paying for something you would not otherwise receive without paying. Everything we buy, we cherish!

It is the giving and receiving exchange of energy that is required to keep a balance for both parties. Givers respect yourself enough to value what you are giving. Receivers respect and value the energy of what the other person is giving to you back in the best way you can.

If this exchange is not present and the energy between parties begins to be effected the art of expression through communication is essential.

I always like to use an example of a catch up lunch or dinner with you and a friend. Was this another time that you or the other party paid for the meal? Have you reciprocated back or offered? Reflect on the conversation. Was it one sided and just drained your energy to do all the listening and supporting without being heard yourself? Did you do all the talking and not ask your friend how they are doing? Or did you both come away from the meal knowing, learning and supporting each other equally?

E = Expression

"The art of communication is the language of leadership"

— James Humes

Expression is perhaps the most important skill to embrace.

Communication is everything. Without it we cannot have relationship with others. We cannot understand others. Others cannot understand us. We express our needs and wants and what we don't want through communication. We learn about others through communication. When we don't communicate, how can we expect anyone to know us or understand us?

Once I opened up to my internal truth, accepting myself fully, living in gratitude for all that was coming my way including communication and understanding the importance of the equal giving and receiving in communication, I then started communicating my truth and vulnerabilities very openly and asked for communication I needed back. There is power in sharing and communicating vulnerably or transparently. Because you share openly, a connection is made, a trust is formed, healing and helping of yourself and others is created, and people start to gravitate towards you because you are being real. However your truth may not always be easy to hear or communicate. Sometimes people don't always understand, agree, or align with you, and that is ok too. Though what I learned was the importance of setting the communication free anyway. Without a place to go, the lack of conversing will either implode or create a sense of loneliness because you are not being heard.

How we express ourselves and how we communicate is important to be conscious of. How is your tone, body language, emotions during communication? Are you telling someone what to do vs asking or suggesting? Are you engaging a conversation or are you always wanting to be "right"? Are you communicating or trying to communicate as effectively as possible, that allows the other person or persons to be in a place to listen or respond and understand.

Pay attention to how you receive communication from others. Are you actively listening? Do you only have half your attention there? Do you respond or react in judgement, fear, lack of acceptance or understanding of the other party? Or do you respond and react from a place of learning and gratitude for the other party? Effective communication is a give and take on both parties.

No response is a response. What message are we giving others when we don't respond? While it may not be intentional, life can get busy yes, if we forget to respond to someone even if it is weeks later, it is best to acknowledge forgetting to respond rather than leaving a possible impression to the other party that they were ignored, that you are not keeping your word, or that they are not important. Better yet, if you know in the moment you are tied up, avoid the lack of response by telling them that you're going to be busy for the next day or two or even the next few hours and you'll get back to them at a certain point in time. If it is an intentional lack of response because of an area you are not comfortable responding to or a conversation you feel is going to be difficult to have, it's important to let that person know authentically where you are and how you're feeling so the other party knows that you're not avoiding them or ignoring them and there is no confusion behind the lack of response. Then get back to them when you feel ready to express that part of yourself and be open to having that conversation with them. Or possibly you need to tell them you prefer not to be in communication with them anymore, and explain why.

To assist with the above, and to receive communication you are seeking in general, it is up to you to ask for the communication you need to receive. Reminder to opposite party, respond in best way you can as mentioned above. It is always best to ask, if you are not getting what you need, so you are not carrying the energy of the unknown, which can create all kinds of unhealthy mind-sets.

Where are you holding back communication because you feel you may not be heard or accepted in a certain way?

Do you manipulate conversations so you can be heard, seen, and accepted in a certain way because you feel you wouldn't be if you stayed true to your-self and spoke authentically? Why don't you speak your truth? What are you afraid of others hearing?

Never ever assume anything of anyone or any situation. Always Ask. You never know how one thing may appear on the outside, may be a totally different story on the inside. Assumptions can lead to lack of communication and therefore lack of clarity or truth around a situation or the person.

Are you just waiting for someone to communicate something to you? Are you assuming that someone is going to tell you something that you are waiting to hear? This can cause a lot of internal conflict, as well, waiting to hear something, not even knowing if it is coming your way. So how we get to shift that is to actually ask someone for the communication that we are seeking. Again, remember that people will either be ready or not ready to have that level of communication with you, and if they're not, be okay with that and allow that conversation to happen when it needs to. Sometimes we think that someone is behaving a certain way or feeling a certain way towards us, but without communication how do we actually know how it is that they're feeling? So, the importance of communication and expressing ourselves is something I can't stress enough.

How another person responds to us is not what we get to focus on. If they respond back in reactionary tone or a judgment of some sort, we get to remember, again, that people are sitting in their own moment of learning and truth. Accept where they are. How they react has nothing to do with you. We all get to control how we react. We can however, in taking responsibility for our part in the communication, take their reaction as feedback. Were we communicating in a certain way that did not produce an effective response from the other party? How could we have communicated differently if so?

Feedback is a vital form of communication something I have learned to embrace and ask for routinely by those in my life. Feedback is the sharing of an experience someone has had with you whether "good" or "bad". It helps to keep us conscious of who we are being and how we are being perceived, so we can continue to learn, grow and be the best that we can for ourselves and others. Asking for feedback is just as important as listening to it when it comes to us unknowingly. Take a look at how you're creating a particular experience for the other person. How can you keep up the same positive vibe? Or what shifts can you make to ensure a better experience with someone? What are you learning about yourself through this constructive feedback?

Always do the best you can to conscious-ly communicate. Listen to each other's truths, accept one another for where they are, be thankful for the conversa-tion and knowledge gained, remember to equally give and receive in the conversa-tion, then let it all be knowing that you have expressed yourself fully in that moment as you best knew how or could.

A wonderful example is during dinner one night with friends and their daughter. Two things happened. One, I noticed very quickly the dynamic between husband and wife and how their communication with each other was hindering their best experience of each other. Two, school difficulties were coming up in conversation with their daughter. With permission, we addressed the lack of active listening and rush to react in conversation, without embracing the perspective of the spouse that was limiting effective communi-cation and understanding within the mar-riage; I was able to communicate with their daughter my experiences of being bullied in school growing up and how to use these steps I'm sharing here to help her mindset shift now, instead of allowing it to affect her later. The couple came away remembering the strengths and love of one another, the daughter went from not wanting to go back to school to deal with these challenges, to be-

ing ready to face the other students in a dif-
ferent light, standing in her truth and accept-
ing herself fully. Beautiful! What can you
share or how can you shift your communica-
tion to create more peace?

D = Detachment

"The root of suffering is attachment"

- Buddha

Let it go!

What is detachment? It is the practice of letting go of an attachment to something, someone, or a situation.

This is really the process of surrendering to the divine and trusting life to flow the way that it is supposed to flow because when we try and control something or when we are expecting something to happen in a certain way, we actually block the flow of how it's actually supposed to be done or how it's actually supposed to be created and in the time that it's supposed to be created.

Detaching for me was going into meditation or prayer, asking my God source and Angels to help me, guide me or bring in what it is that I was seeking. I would continue to work on it on my behalf while allowing the universe to work alongside with me and literally let it go, knowing all would manifest itself in divine timing. The moment we put worry, expectation or controlling energy on it, the process slows itself down. When we start to trust and accept that all things are being done for our higher good we then start to let go and allow the flow. When I began to practice this process of detachment, and I allowed things to manifest as they were, I kid you not, every single time that I have done this, things have manifested themselves in perfect time, order, and perfectly how it was supposed to be. If any of it manifested earlier or later, the situation or myself would not have been ready for it at that time.

We do not know what, when, why and how something is supposed to be. I say when we put expectation on something we block the flow of what is meant to be from actually happening. The moment we let go, we return to peace, release any pressure or anxiety towards it and that's when the magic and manifestation happen!

Detaching from people, situations or experiences are also an important practice. We remember that all people, things and experiences have come our way to help us learn and grow. All is on purpose for a purpose. Once the learning and growth has reached its mark, it may not be something, someone, or an experience we need to have anymore. If we lose something or someone, or a situation or relationship has ended, be thankful for what you have gained from it, how it has served you, how you have served it and be ready and excited for the next experience coming your way, because you now can be open to bigger and better experiences and growth.

We create a new found love for all universal beings and attributes around us because without it our life would not unfold perfectly as it has been. (And life is unfolding perfectly for you, always remember the growth you are experiencing along the way moving you further into your purpose and enlightenment)

Moving to the Bay Area from Los Angeles, a city I am so connected to that my heart and soul cherish, a life that was heavenly, was a challenge for me. Once I felt the call to move to be closer to family and serve the community here through my healing and coaching practice, I made a conscious effort to detach to how all would turn out. I had to start from scratch. I let go and trusted the universe had my back. I prayed for the best outcomes, got to work, and in less than a year, I've written this book, my business has doubled its size than it was able in LA, I have multiple agencies I assist through my degrees and certifications and life has become full. What will you choose to let go of and allow the doors to open for you?

U = Unconditional Love

"Love each other as I have loved you"

- John 15:12

Now, here's the thing about this that's so interesting. I've always been the one, my whole life, to literally love on people and I literally love life and all it offers! Though as mentioned in the beginning, I was living a darker side within myself. What I learnt was that while I was loving on everybody else, I wasn't loving myself.

When we don't love our self we then operate in fear of ourselves or ego because we want to show up as "perfect". Mostly to be validated and accepted by others.

When we love ourselves we operate knowing we are already perfect, there is no fear/ego, just peace. Peace within ourselves and for/with others. We carry ourselves with grace, respect, and ease.

After I awoke to God's presence in my life and knew within myself that I was a child of God and that God's source is actually in me and that God's source is actually in everybody, I really started to embrace us all as brothers and sisters and his children. Not only are we all connected, but everything is connected. Not only are we created on purpose for a purpose, so is literally everything else! Everything on this planet, everything in this world is connected. Here to serve one another. Think of how the sun, the moon, the stars, nature, animals (really you can insert anything here) make you feel physically or emotionally. Without one thing or another we wouldn't have certain functions and luxuries of life. This is universal love! All I could see, was love for everybody and everything. When people were in their worst forms with me or I was watching them be in their worst forms with others, all I could see for them was love. Love that they needed. Love that was already inside of them, that they just didn't see yet for themselves.

Here's another thing. While we can choose to see everyone though the eyes of love, we can also stay true to loving, honoring, and respecting ourselves when others are not. If someone does something harmful towards you or to another, remember that they know not what they do. It is not personal. These are still people who are in a stage of life where they're reacting based on their personal experiences, learning, and growth. They not yet have the peace within themselves. You can send them light and love on their journey while also holding them accountable for actions that were otherwise respectable to you or another person. This is actually a way of unconditionally loving and honoring yourself or the others that were effected, yet it is also expressing love towards the offender. How? Because you are helping them take accountability for their actions, that without, one cannot grow, learn and become their victorious self. You are helping someone take responsibility for their life, for that one can be grateful.

That's just what I started doing. If I was in conversation with someone, friends, patients, clients, or even strangers and they would be in some sort of state of distress, I would simply say something that was beautiful about them and helped them become aware of that to help shift their mindset and thought process. You can't see any sort of hate, anger, judgment or resentment towards anybody when you choose to focus on all the good qualities about somebody. You also can not see any hate, anger, judgement about yourself or jealousy towards others when you truly start to embrace and love your unique self. The only person you are really competing with is you. The process of living through unconditional love, really seeing yourself and everybody through the eyes of love, helps to shift perspective to peace that everyone and everything is really okay just where we are.

God has created everything perfectly and directly for each of us and each thing to benefit off of. There are no accidents or mistakes.

The practice of seeing everything through the eyes of love is a fun experience for me. I cut a fruit and there is a heart. Anywhere I walk or anywhere I look a heart shows up. I move a cup and the watermark has formed a heart. If you take a look at the cover photo of this book, through all the water around me, under my right foot it is dry in shape of a heart. The same day of that photo shoot, the seaweed showed up in forms of hearts. I literally have a photo album saved of all the "random" hearts that show up. My heart is so full. What can you find more love in? Where can you let more love in?

R = Responsibility

"My life and business changed when I stopped making others responsible for my happiness or success"

— Ritika Rose

A great quote that came out of a challenge I did when asked what was the moment when it all changed.

Through the journey of these steps and the mindset shifts I allowed myself to embrace, I truly was starting to live my best life.

Becoming the leader of your own life means taking responsibility for your own life, your own happiness, what you're creating and who you're being. Stay in your truth. Don't let anybody else shift or shape who you are. Remember that you're created for a purpose on purpose, and only you can do what you do, only you can be who you are. You are a unique creation. Always follow what feels right to you—that is your responsibility.

The moment you start allowing other people to dictate what is right or wrong in your world and how your world should be or how you should be in the world, then we immediately fall into a level of inauthenticity which then creates the lack of happiness, peace, joy and bliss within us. So remember to stay true to yourself and what feels right to you in your gut and in your heart, accepting yourself for who you are unconditionally.

Remember that every person and every situation serves a purpose that comes along our path. It's being sent in front of us and into our path for a reason. What do we learn from everything that's being brought to or taken away from us? What did that person or situation teach you about yourself? How are you stronger? How do you love yourself more? What are you ready to take on now?

If there is some reason in life that you're feeling unhappy, stressed, not joyful, or not peaceful internally, consider the steps I've laid out before you. Which of these skills were you not following on daily basis?

Remember no one and nothing is perfect. No one person and no one thing can "make you happy". You must fall in love with yourself and your life first. That is where the true inner happiness, peace and joy lie. If life falls short and starts feeling down, it's ok. We may forget to follow these steps at times. Don't judge or be hard on yourself or others. Acknowledge it. Retrace these steps. Love yourself for where you are and where you are growing! Take those thoughts of self-rejection or social rejection and shift them in to ejection. Ejection to you Freedom, Power, Truth.

I remember the time I felt like I was just going through the motions of life and feel so beyond grateful for the mentors, personal and spiritual development workshops, books, conscious individuals and groups that came my way. I allowed myself to explore deeper levels of myself and feel so incredibly blessed to be in a position to now do the same for others. Sometimes it takes a breakdown to have a breakthrough, other times you know you need a breakthrough and it's your responsibility to ask and get the support/help you need before you breakdown. Follow a mentor. Work with a coach. Take the steps towards your personal growth and connecting to your higher self.

IT = Internal Transformation

Today, I show up in the world ok being my true authentic self, real, honest, highly conscious and aware of myself and others. I show up balanced. I show up peaceful. I show up positive. I show up with love, love of myself and love of others in such a deep way. I show up fully accepting, forgiving and accountable to myself, my actions and others, as well as, the world around me and what it is presenting. Allowing things to flow but also taking responsibility for when I feel like it's not in flow and making sure I take the steps and use the skills that I learned in order to rebalance anything taking away my peace, or developing unhealthy stress or unhappiness that I'm feeling.

How do you want to show up? Which of these steps can you start putting into practice or learn more about?

I have accepted and become grateful for all the experiences that I went through as a child and growing up, because everything was a lesson to make me stronger. It was to help me understand and connect with what other people may be going through and the people that I'm serving today in my practice. Everything that I've gone through in my life was in divine order for me to be able to really understand and to see people for the truth of who they are. To be able to serve them in a way that's unconditional, to help them to also see the beauty that's within themselves and help them understand their growth and their lessons to help them be conscious of their purpose. If I had not gone through the internal transformation myself, I wouldn't be able to do the work I've been guided to do today and make big changes in people's lives by helping them transform into the true being that they're meant to be.

What transformations would you like to make?

By using the principles of TAGGED UR IT, you will shift from feeling lost, confused or trapped in the world that you're living in today into your personal freedom, power and truth. It will secure peace and joy that you can have in every present moment in your daily life.

You are the only one with your purpose. It is up to you to lead it. You are the only one living your life. It is your responsibility to own it. You are the only one that will ever create internally lasting peace, love, and happiness. So commit to yourself now to Become the Leader of Your Own Life.

With Gratitude, Peace, and Blessings

RiTika Rose

A few praises:

"Every time I work with you I walk away with new peace, clarity, and understanding. Amazing!

- Shannon, Financial advisor

"Ritika provides excellent feedback, direction, and help to feel grounded while moving in a fast paced environment. Highly recommend her. Excellent ability to get straight to the matter. There is confirmation along the way that is spot on!! What a gift."

- Robin, High Tech/Healthcare

"Ritika is a deeply caring individual who helped me take the right actions and find a path in what seemed to be my chaotic life. She listens well and helped me to come to the most empowering solution to take action."

- L. Pearson, Author/Entrepreneur

"I am so grateful to have found Ritika. I have spent years in traditional therapy with little success. In just a few months with Ritika, my whole life has changed! I am calmer, and now have direction, which I never had before. I have so much relief now, and it's all because of her. Words cannot express the eternal gratitude I have for Ritika's help."

- Stacey, Teacher

"Expect to feel empowered, clear, supported, and on the road to major healing on all energetic levels."

- Azure, M.S.W; Reiki Master

"When I feel I'm getting off my path in life, I connect with Ritika and I feel so inspired after and accomplish so much."

- Elmira, Artist

"With Ritika's guidance I was able to let go of a false belief that no longer served me. Since this healing I've been manifesting and attracting exactly what I need on my path. If you are looking to release any blocks that you may be facing, and find spiritual guidance from someone with a pure intention to serve, uplift and help you step into your light and true power Ritika is the right mentor for you!"

- Yvonne, Model/Business Coach

Respecting clients privacy, first name or initial are used based on each client's permissions.

www.ritikarose.com

Made in the USA
Middletown, DE
19 January 2018